COLORADO
SCENIC SPLENDOR

Roger Edrinn
Photographs and Text

COLORADO
SCENIC SPLENDOR SERIES

Mount Ypsilon

Winter alpenglow lights the summit of Mount Ypsilon, 13,514 feet, in
Rocky Mountain National Park.

Mount Wilson

Summer alpenglow turns the foreground rocks fire-red as the overhead cloud deck gradually reduces the sun light on Mount Wilson, 14,246 feet, in the Lizard Head Wilderness.

FOREWORD

Welcome to Colorado Scenic Splendor. In its pages I have endeavored to create a diverse scenic presentation of Colorado. You will find snow-capped mountains as well as delicate flowers among its varied offerings. When possible these are combined to put Colorado into perspective. At the end of the book, one page is devoted to a discussion of selected photographs.

Prior to 1993 I had only published photographs of Colorado's Fourteeners, the mountains above 14,000 feet. While these 54 mountains represent some of the most scenic subjects in Colorado, I found them constraining. They limited my photographic possibilities to the same 54 mountains. Because of this limitation I sought other avenues of photographic expression. In late 1993, two other photographers, Todd Caudle and David Dahms, and I collaborated on an engagement calendar. That event was like opening the flood gates. Instantly, any and all Colorado subjects were available to me and my camera. In early 1994 I set out on a mission to photograph all of Colorado, corner to corner and bottom to top. With each photo trip I found more and more of

Colorado's beauty. My photographic skills rapidly increased as more and varied subjects challenged my eye and technique. I now have in excess of 20,000 images from which to draw upon for various books and calendars. My Colorado quest is still a work in progress with no end in sight. An interesting and unexpected benefit of this photo productivity was that I had renewed enthusiasm for the Fourteeners.

In addition to creating the photographs, doing the book design and layout brings me a great deal of artistic satisfaction. For example, contemplate the photos as they are matched across two pages. Considerable thought went into the visual harmony of each photo pair. Geographic diversity was a further goal in my selection process. I did this to emphasize the continuity of images across different regions of Colorado. This level of product integrity is seldom acheived by publishing factories.

When I was a consumer of other people's photographs, I always felt cheated when I found the same photo repeated over and over in different books and calendars. Now that I am a creator of fine photographs and publications, I vow to never short change my readers. I emphasize this because I want you to be assured you can always expect fresh images showing the multifaceted splendor of Colorado.

Roger Edrinn

Selected products featuring photographer Roger Edrinn:

Books:
Fourteeners – A Photo Journey
Colorado – Scenic Splendor
Colorado – Mountain Reflections

Calendars:
Fourteeners (Wall)
The Beauty of Colorado (Desk/Wall)

Posters:
Fourteeners (photo collage)
Maroon Bells – Autumn
Maroon Bells – Winter
Longs Peak – Diamond
Mount of the Holy Cross

Front Cover – Western wallflowers carpet the valley below the snow-capped Sangre de Cristo Range.

Title Page – Alpine sunflowers decorate a ridge with Colorado's highest, Mount Elbert and Mount Massive, in the distance.

Back Cover – Heavy clouds cause only the ridge tops of the Never Summer Range to be lit, Rocky Mountain National Park.

Above The Timber

Fort Collins, Colorado

Published by: Above the Timber
2366 Wapiti Road
Fort Collins, CO 80525-3512

ISBN: 1-881059-31-6

Printed in Korea

Holy Cross Wilderness

In the warm glow of sunset, marsh marigolds line a small pool at the headwaters of Cross Creek. Savage Peak, 13,139 feet, can be seen through the saddle of Missouri Pass.

Sawatch Sunset

The setting sun plays a spectrum of red-orange light on the clouds above the silhouetted Sawatch Range.

Lost Trail Creek

Indian paintbrush appear as so many multicolored popsicles in a meadow above the East Fork of Lost Trail Creek in the Maroon Bells–Snowmass Wilderness.

Avalanche Creek

High above Avalanche Creek, a cluster of alpine avens soften the alpine domain in the Maroon Bells–Snowmass Wilderness. The tall peak in the foreground is Mount Richey, 12,400 feet. In the distance, at the far right are the twin summits of Mount Sopris, 12,953 feet.

Lily Pad Lake

Blue skies and puffy clouds play off the surface amid flowering water lilies.
Lily Pad Lake is at 11,100 feet in the White River National Forest.

Rabbit Ears Peak

The Continental Divide meanders through Colorado, frequently crossing craggy peaks high above the timber. Near Rabbit Ears Pass, the terrain is timbered, soft and rolling. The actual "line" of the Divide is between the camera and Rabbit Ears Peak, 10,654 feet.

Savage Peak

Rising above Missouri Lakes Basin, Savage Peak, 13,139 feet, displays its summer splendor. This is the second largest of the four Missouri Lakes in the Holy Cross Wilderness.

Tijeras Peak

A rocky side pool of Lower Sand Creek Lake reflects golden light from Tijeras Peak, 13,604 feet. Both by its character and elevation, the peak is one of the most prominent summits in the Sangre de Cristo Range.

Fish Creek Falls

Filled with the rush of a heavy snowmelt, Fish Creek Falls is a popular recreation site in the Routt National Forest east of Steamboat Springs.

Quartz Creek Beaver Ponds

The high summits of the Sawatch Range are covered by autumn's first snowfall. North Quartz Creek drains south from Cumberland Pass in the Gunnison National Forest.

Grenadier Range

Swirling clouds obscure, Peak Two, 13,475 feet, as a nearby mountain lake is
bathed in sunlight. The Grenadiers are among the most remote mountains in
the vast Weminuche Wilderness in southwest Colorado.

Heart Lake

The "weather gods" scowl above Heart Lake at sunset. The lake is situated on the White River Plateau north of Glenwood Canyon.

Sawatch Panorama

Some of Colorado's highest summits que up in snow-capped splendor. At the far left is Mount Columbia, 14,073 feet; La Plata Peak, 14,336 feet, anchors the far right.

Never Summer Wilderness

Columbine thrive on thin cliff-side shelves just a few feet below the
Continental Divide. The Divide follows this ridge, then turns right over
Baker Pass, 11,200 feet, and along the volcanic peaks in the Never Summer
Wilderness.

Lizard Head Wilderness

Two nearly identical scenes separated by more than 200 miles. Colorado's state flower, the columbine, nests in a sunlit perch below Lizard Head, 13,113 feet. The remnant of a volcanic chimney, the peak separates the San Juan and Uncompahgre National Forests.

Colorado National Monument

Rabbitbrush thrive on the thin, dry soils typically found on the Uncompahgre Plateau. Independence Monument stands majestic above the Grand Valley.

Great Sand Dunes National Monument

Rabbitbrush occupy a sandy perch above Medano Creek. The 100 yard
wide creek is only inches deep. Beyond rise the dunes.

McClellan Mountain

The rocky summit ridge glows on a mid-summer morning. At the far right
Grays Peak, 14,270 feet, is the highest point on the Continental Divide in
the United States.

Collier Mountain

A late summer sunset illuminates the golden tundra. Collier Mountain is on
the Continental Divide in the Arapaho National Forest.

Lake Catamount

A verdant landscape of trees and grasses surround Lake Catamount in the Yampa River Valley. The Flat Tops are the snow-capped mountains in the distance.

Illinois River

A heavy spring snowpack coupled with warm summer days causes the meandering Illinois River to ignore its channel in North Park. Seen here below the distant Rabbit Ears Range, the Illinois is one of many feeder streams of the North Platte River.

San Luis Valley Sunrise

The rising sun behind the distant Culebra Range paints the sky and surface
of Smith Reservoir in the San Luis Valley.

Sunset Splendor

As the evening sun drops behind clouds, shafts of light silhouette spruce trees near Corona Pass. Once a wagon and train route over the Continental Divide, the pass is west of Boulder.

Sangre de Cristo Range

Bright yellow western wallflowers seem to stretch forever in the Wet Mountain Valley. The snow-capped summits of the Sangre de Cristo Range combine with the flowers to define Colorado's scenic splendor.

29

Dinosaur National Monument

In Echo Park, the waters of the Yampa River join the Green River. Sandy
side pools reflect the north end of the massive Steamboat Rock formation.

Conejos Peak

Mix Lake is like a little gem hiding among the spruce below Conejos Peak,
13,172 feet. The lake is in the Rio Grande National Forest.

Treasure Vault Lake

As seen from Missouri Pass, Treasure Vault Lake occupies a high bench
above Cross Creek. The distant snow-capped ridge is dominated by Middle
Mountain, 12,618, in the Holy Cross Wilderness.

Collegiate Peaks Panorama

A vista provided by a knob on South Peak, three of the five Collegiate
Peaks are visible. From left to right are Mount Columbia, 14,073 feet,
Mount Harvard, 14,420 feet, and Mount Oxford, 14,153 feet.

Hurricane Peak

Above 10,000 feet in the Colorado Rockies, winter can appear during any month. This late-September view of Hurricane Peak, 13,447 feet, shows an overnight transition from brown to white.

Hayden Spire

A high, thick deck of clouds, a thinner lower haze, and the setting sun combine to create a golden veil around the spire. Hayden Spire can be viewed from Forest Canyon Overlook in Rocky Mountain National Park.

Tranquil Waters

Reflections of puffy clouds scattered across the morning sky collect on the mirror surface of a mountain pond. Located inside the Maroon Bells–Snowmass Wilderness, the pond is along the Hell Roaring Trail.

Milwaukee Peak

Upper Sand Creek Lake sits on a glacier-sculpted bench below Milwaukee
Peak, 13,522 feet. Sand Creek and its lakes are in the Sangre de Cristo
Wilderness, on the west side of Music Pass.

Nellie Creek Falls

Golden aspen frame one of the prettiest falls in Colorado. The falls are located in the Uncompahgre National Forest west of Lake City.

Red Oak and Golden Aspen

The rolling hills along the East Fork of Dallas Creek are covered with gambel oak and quaking aspen. Each autumn they change hues below the snow-covered Sneffels Range.

Cimarron Sunset

Chimney Rock and Courthouse Mountain are set ablaze by a February sunset. Cimarron Ridge is east of Ridgway in the Uncompahgre National Forest.

Beckwith Mountains
Above mile after mile of rolling aspen forest, the Beckwith Mountains
dominate this view west of Kebler Pass in the Gunnison National Forest.

Weminuche Wilderness

Tundra pools, volcanic faces, and scattered clouds reflect a September sunset.
At 492,418 acres, the Weminuche is Colorado's largest wilderness area.

Mountain Grandeur

A snow-dusted mountain framed by a blue sky with silhouetted spruce seem to sing together in joy: 'Tis a delight to be in Colorado. It's a typical scene along Clear Creek in the San Isabel National Forest.

Meadow Mountain

The emerald green slopes of Meadow Mountain combine with snowfields and buff-colored rock to create an inviting walk-in scene. Imagine sitting on these green slopes in a light breeze, enjoying a summer afternoon in the Maroon Bells–Snowmass Wilderness.

Black Canyon

The steep, dark walls of the Black Canyon are best photographed in overcast light. Viewed from Chasm View Nature Trail on the North Rim, the Gunnison River is but a white thread in the 2,000-foot-deep canyon. Both sides are in the Black Canyon of the Gunnison National Monument.

Cliff Palace

The signature ruins of Mesa Verde National Park, Cliff Palace is easily viewed from across the canyon, or as the many visitors attest, up close and personal.

Stunner Cabin

This stout cabin is the only remaining building in Stunner, once a thriving mining town. Stunner, like so many old settlements, is barely a memory. That which remains is along the Alamosa River in the South San Juan Mountains.

Banker Mine

An airy cabin and ruins sit above the tranquil Clear Creek valley. The Banker Mine is big enough to still be shown on modern maps in the heart of the Sawatch Range.

Buffalo Peaks Sunset

Silhouetted tree tops and towering thunderheads beg to be frozen in time. The locale is the Buffalo Peaks Wilderness at the south end of the Mosquito Range. A name richly deserved for the multitude of the pesky winged critters that live there.

Centennial Peak Sunrise

Low clouds combine with the rising sun to add drama to the La Plata Mountains. The summit of Centennial Peak, 13,062 feet, is partially obscured while its east face blazes with full sunlight.

Medicine Bow Panorama

Lupine tower over common dandelion in this inviting foreground. The Medicine Bow Mountains form an unbroken string, defining the eastern border of North Park.

Pikes Peak and Garden of the Gods

Fresh overnight snow and bright sun cause the eye to alternate between the summit of Pikes Peak and the North Gateway Formation in the Garden of the Gods Park. Notice the Kissing Camels arch on the top left.

Red Mountain No. 1

Bright sun burns off the overnight snowfall to expose the red underlying rock. The reflection of the summit peeks through open water on a semi-frozen pond. Red Mountain No. 1 is located in Colorado's mighty San Juans.

Sunrise Splendor

Delicate pink clouds contrast with a deep blue sky. All is repeated on the surface of Missouri Lake in the Holy Cross Wilderness.

Often I find that my best photographs occur when I place myself in position for good things to happen, and open my mind to what Mother Nature offers. I frequently select a place to photograph by virtue of its uniqueness and my relative lack of photos of the area. I will then either go to the area blind or study maps and select key features I want to view. In any case, the final decision on what to photograph is left to the moment. The following photos are examples of these processes:

Page 3, Mount Wilson: It was late July and I had backpacked up the Cross Mountain Trail with the goal of improving my Mount Wilson portfolio. About 30 minutes before sunrise I hiked along a high ridge to a rocky knob above 12,000 feet. I got out the equipment and anticipated some compositions. This scene occurred about 30 minutes after first light as the clouds began to shadow the summit of Mount Wilson.

Pages 8 and 9, Wilderness Flowers: Two examples of photographs taken in light more than three hours after sunrise. While lacking the warmth of early morning light, both invite the viewer to sit down and enjoy the flowers. Bright colors and beautiful skies can compensate for less than perfect light.

Page 17, Heart Lake: I had never been on the White River Plateau prior to this trip. These dark storm clouds were Mother Nature rewarding me for going to a new locale. The black clouds remind the viewer of their own storm experiences.

Page 28, Smith Reservoir: I positioned myself along the west shore of Smith Reservoir at sundown. Sunset was a disappointment. At sunrise, with tripod and camera, I moved along the shore waiting for the light to develop. A number of strong compositions resulted, making the weak sunset unimportant.

Pages 30 and 31, Sangre de Cristo Flowers: I was driving along Colorado Highway 69 when I noticed these flowers in a field. I stopped at the owner's house to ask permission to photograph the flowers. The owner graciously said yes, and I proceeded to expose about one hundred frames of varying compositions.

THE PHOTOGRAPHS

Page 34, Treasure Vault Lake: I had just hiked over Missouri Pass and finished a light lunch when I began exploring the Cross Creek drainage. The combination of the lake, lacy snowfields, and lone spruce tree made this scene for me. One of the few handheld photos I've taken, made possible by the very bright midday light.

Page 36, Hurricane Peak: To date, the single most productive photo day of my life. The light changed from overcast, to sun, then more snow, all in a matter of minutes. I had a 360 degree panorama of mountains, snow, and tarns resulting in over 400 images.

Pages 42 and 43, Cimarron Ridge: It was a strikingly clear mid-February afternoon when I saw clouds above Cimarron Ridge. I set out from Ridgway and arrived just before sunset. I quickly got my camera and tripod and started climbing a small knob. What I thought would be a good vantage point soon turned out to be knee-deep crusted snow with heavy gambel oak. After seamingly endless breaking through snow, I arrived breathless in a small clearing to get this fading light shot.

Page 53, Centennial Peak: Primarily a photo of negative space with an intensely lighted rock wall to draw the viewer's eye. The transition from fully lit to black took only five minutes.

Page 54 and 55, Medicine Bow Panorama: When I first started working this scene, the North Park mosquitoes greeted me with enthusiasm. I returned to my vehicle and loaded up on repugnant repellent. I then worked the light and flowers for over an hour, getting numerous variations of lupine and light.

Page 60, Ute Ridge Rainbow: It was about two hours before sunset, medium rain, and strong sunlight. These are certain conditions for a rainbow. The trick is to keep camera and film dry when the best light is happening. A wet camera is sometimes the price you pay for such a glorious rainbow.

Back Cover, Never Summer Ridge: It was early morning in Rocky Mountain National Park with snow-covered roads. I had traveled as far east as the Rock Cut, but the heavy overcast turned me back to the west. I stopped at Farview Curve because the view west showed promise. This ridge lit up about ten minutes after I arrived.

I have not discussed cameras, film, or photographic technique for a reason. I find these things to be secondary to the act of being in an opportune place at the moment of best light. While there is never a guarantee good light will happen, you can be assured that nothing great will happen in front of the "tube" doing "one-arm-curls."

Roger Edrinn

Ute Ridge Rainbow

A late afternoon thunderstorm creates one of Mother Nature's most beautiful phenomenon. A 13,000-foot summit on Ute Ridge in the Rio Grande National Forest adds scale to the display.